Quilts
Peaceful Moments

LEISURE ARTS, INC. • Maumelle, Arkansas

Meet the Designer:
Tricia Cribbs

Tricia Cribbs of Turning Twenty® (formerly FriendFolks) has been a top-selling quilt designer and lecturer for more than 20 years. Creating impressive quilts that are surprisingly simple to piece and quick to complete is her signature style. Tricia finishes her quilts with beautiful freehand machine quilting that resembles the intricate hand stitching found on antique quilts.

"As far back as I can remember, I busied myself creating beautiful things," she recalls. "I sorted through colorful scraps left over from mama's dressmaking to sew clothes for my dolls. My maternal grandmother taught me to crochet and embroider when I was 9 years old, and I still love to sit and embroider for hours on end."

After marrying her high school sweetheart at the age of 18, Tricia turned to sewing clothing for herself and eventually her daughter and son. The height of her sewing experience was making a beaded wedding gown for her daughter.

"In 1980, I was bitten by the not-so-rare, but life-changing, quilt bug," she says. "In time I began to create my own designs and found tremendous satisfaction in my work. In 1994, I purchased my first longarm quilting machine and taught myself how to just let go and quilt FREESTYLE! What fun!"

With the help of her husband, Gary, Tricia soon had a successful pattern business and quilt shop called FriendFolks. She was also designing buttons and whimsical fabrics. "By 2013," she says, "our company had become known as 'The Turning Twenty' people [because of her book series by that name], so we officially changed our name." Tricia also lectures and holds quilting workshops. More information may be found on her website, TurningTwenty.com.

Introduction

Fanciful fabrics, captivating color schemes, and cherished designs — you'll find them all in this heartwarming quilting guide. Six traditional patterns are easy for beginners to piece, yet the clever combinations of colors and shapes will delight even the most experienced quilter. "Back in the Saddle" and "Remember When" highlight playful designs and faux-vintage prints. Choose "Double Irish Chain" for a bit of rustic elegance. "Church in the Wildwood" and "Simple Circles" feature eye-catching details, while "Pineapple Delight" offers a fresh twist on a classic pattern. Best of all, easy-to-follow instructions and gorgeous photographs make these timeless treasures oh-so simple to create.

Table of Contents

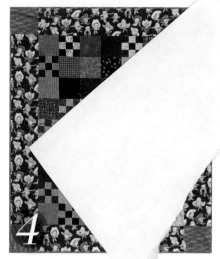

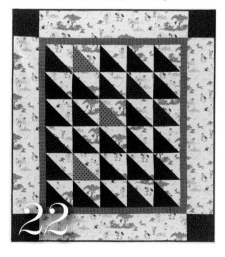
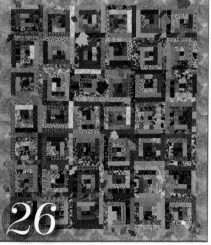

Back in the Saddle

Featuring faux denim corners and a cowboy print border, this lively throw promises a real Western adventure. Choose plaids and masculine prints for a quilt your favorite fellow will love.

Pieced by Patty Hawkins.
Finished Block Size: 6" x 6" (15 cm x 15 cm)
Finished Quilt Size: 59" x 71" (150 cm x 180 cm)

YARDAGE REQUIREMENTS

Yardage is based on 43"/44" (109 cm/112 cm) wide fabric with a usable width of 40" (102 cm).

- 1⅝ yds (1.5 m) **total** of assorted prints for Block A
- 1⅜ yds (1.3 m) **total** of assorted dark prints for Block B
- 1⅜ yds (1.3 m) **total** of assorted light prints for Block B
- 2½ yds (2.3 m) of border print
- ⅜ yd (34 cm) of print fabric for corner squares
- 4½ yds (4.1 m) of backing fabric
- ⅝ yd (57 cm) of binding fabric
- 67" x 79" (170 cm x 201 cm) piece of batting

CUTTING OUT THE PIECES

*All measurements include ¼" seam allowances. Follow **Rotary Cutting**, page 31, to cut fabric. Cutting lengths given for borders are exact.*

From assorted prints:
- Cut 46 squares (**A**) 6½" x 6½" for Block A.

From dark prints:
For **each** Block B:
- Cut 1 strip 2½" wide. From this strip, cut 2 rectangles (**B**) 2½" x 6" and 1 square (**C**) 2½" x 2½".

From light prints:
For **each** Block B:
- Cut 1 strip 2½" wide. From this strip, cut 1 rectangle (**D** 2½" x 6" and 2 squares (**E**) 2½" x 2½".

From border print:
- Cut 2 *crosswise* top/bottom borders (**G**) 8½" x 42½", pieced as needed.
- Cut 2 *lengthwise* side borders (**F**) 8½" x 54½".

From print fabric for corner squares:
- Cut 1 strip 8½" wide. From this strip, cut 4 corner squares (**H**) 8½" x 8½".

From binding fabric:
- Cut 7 strips 2½" wide.

MAKING THE BLOCKS

*Follow **Piecing** and **Pressing**, page 32, to make the nine patch blocks.*

Block B

1. Sew 2 dark print rectangles (**B**) and 1 light print rectangle (**D**) together as shown to make **Strip Set A**. Make 17 **Strip Set A's** from assorted prints. Cut across **Strip Set A's** at 2¹/₂" intervals to make **Unit 1**. Make 34 Unit 1's (2 for each **Block B**).

Strip Set A   **Unit 1**
(make 17)   (make 34)

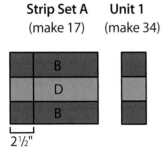

2. Using the same 2 prints, sew 1 dark print square (**C**) and 2 light print squares (**E**) together as shown to make **Unit 2**. Make 17 **Unit 2's** (1 for each **Block B**).

Unit 2
(make 17)

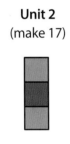

3. Sew 2 **Unit 1's** and 1 **Unit 2** together as shown to make **Block B**. Make 17 **Block B's**.

Block B Diagram
(make 17)

ASSEMBLING THE QUILT TOP

*Refer to photo, page 5, and **Quilt Top Diagram** for placement.*

1. Sew 5 **Block A's** and 2 **Block B's** together in random order to make **Row A**. Make 6 **Row A's**.
2. Sew 6 **Block A's** and 1 **Block B** together in random order to make **Row B**. Make 2 **Row B's**.
3. Sew 4 **Block A's** and 3 **Block B's** together in random order to make **Row C**.
4. Sew **Rows A-C** together in random order to make **Quilt Top Center**.

ADDING THE BORDERS

For all borders, match centers and corners and ease in fullness.

1. Sew side borders (**F**) to **Quilt Top Center**.
2. Sew 1 corner square (**H**) to each end of top and bottom borders (**G**) to make 2 **Border Units**.
3. Sew a **Border Unit** to the top and bottom of **Quilt Top Center** to make quilt top.

COMPLETING THE QUILT

1. Follow **Quilting**, page 34, to mark, layer, and quilt as desired. Our quilt was machine quilted.
2. Follow **Making Straight-Grain Binding**, page 37, to make 7⁵/₈ yds of 2¹/₂"w binding.
3. Follow **Attaching Binding with Mitered Corners**, page 37, to attach binding to quilt.

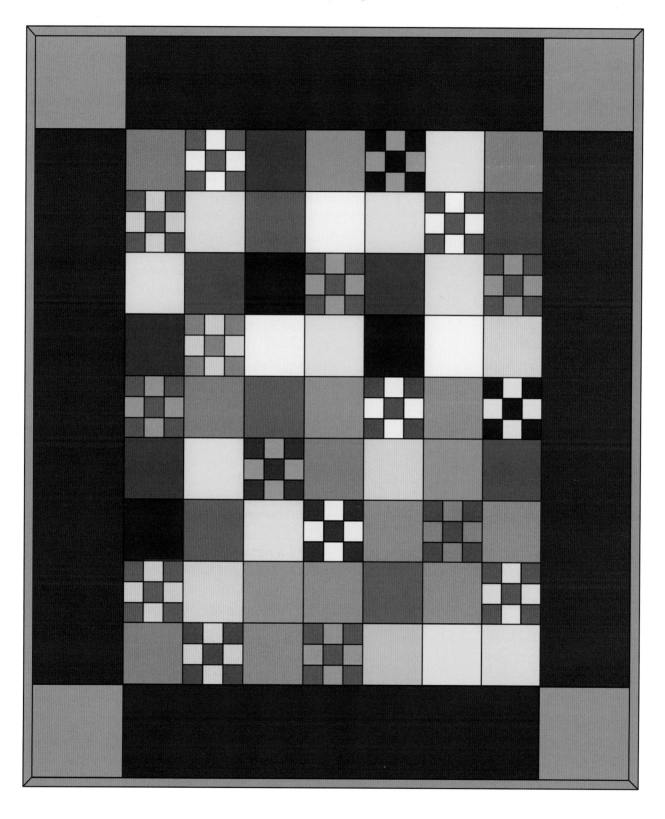

Pineapple Delight

A favorite motif for generations, the pineapple symbolizes hospitality and generosity. And what guest wouldn't feel welcome when you pamper them with this delightfully refreshing quilt?

Finished Block Size: 11$^1/_2$ " x 11$^1/_2$" (29 cm x 29 cm)
Finished Quilt Size: 101$^1/_2$" x 101$^1/_2$" (258 cm x 258 cm)

YARDAGE REQUIREMENTS

Yardage is based on 43"/44" (109 cm/112 cm) wide fabric with a usable width of 40" (102 cm).

    10$^1/_4$ yds (9.4 m) of white print fabric
    6$^3/_8$ yds (5.8 m) of blue print fabric
    2$^7/_8$ yds (2.6 m) of rose print fabric
    6$^5/_8$ yds (6.1 m) of floral print fabric
    9$^1/_4$ yds (8.5 m) of backing fabric
    $^7/_8$ yd (80 cm) of binding fabric
    110" x 110" (279 cm x 279 cm) piece of batting

You will also need:
    Fabric glue stick

CUTTING OUT THE PIECES

*All measurements include $^1/_4$" seam allowances. Follow **Rotary Cutting**, page 31, to cut fabric. Cutting lengths given for borders are exact.*

From white print fabric:
- Cut 114 strips 2$^1/_4$" wide. From these strips, cut 256 rectangles (**No. 2**) 2$^1/_4$" x 2$^3/_4$", 256 rectangles (**No. 6**) 2$^1/_4$" x 5$^3/_4$", and 256 rectangles (**No. 8**) 2$^1/_4$" x 6$^3/_4$".
- Cut 2 *lengthwise* middle side borders (**C**) 2" x 95".
- Cut 2 *lengthwise* middle top/bottom borders (**D**) 2" x 98".

From remaining width:
- Cut 37 strips 2$^1/_4$" wide. From these strips, cut 256 rectangles (**No. 4**) 2$^1/_4$" x 4$^1/_2$".

From blue print fabric:
- Cut 38 strips 2$^1/_4$" wide. From these strips, cut 128 rectangles (**No. 5**) 2$^1/_4$" x 5 " and 128 rectangles (**No. 7**) 2$^1/_4$" x 5$^3/_4$".
- Cut 6 strips 1$^5/_8$" wide. From these strips, cut 11 strips (**G**) 1$^5/_8$" x 20" for strip sets.
- Cut 2 *lengthwise* outer side borders (**E**) 2" x 98".
- Cut 2 *lengthwise* outer top/bottom borders (**F**) 2" x 101".

From remaining width:
- Cut 51 strips 2$^1/_4$" wide. From these strips, cut 128 rectangles (**No. 3**) 2$^1/_4$" x 4$^1/_4$" and 128 rectangles (**No. 9**) 2$^1/_4$" x 6$^3/_4$".

From rose print fabric:
- Cut 2 *lengthwise* inner side borders (**A**) $1^3/_4$" x $92^1/_2$".
- Cut 2 *lengthwise* inner top/bottom borders (**B**) $1^3/_4$" x 95".

  From remaining width:
- Cut 19 strips $2^1/_2$" wide. From these strips, cut 128 rectangles (**No. 10**) $2^1/_2$" x $4^1/_4$".

From floral print fabric:
- Cut 79 strips $2^1/_4$" wide. From these strips, cut 128 rectangles (**No. 3**) $2^1/_4$" x $4^1/_4$", 128 rectangles (**No. 5**) $2^1/_4$" x 5", 128 rectangles (**No. 7**) $2^1/_4$" x $5^3/_4$", and 128 rectangles (**No. 9**) $2^1/_4$" x $6^3/_4$".
- Cut 15 strips $2^1/_2$" wide. From these strips, cut 128 rectangles (**No. 10**) $2^1/_2$" x $4^1/_4$".
- Cut 6 strips $1^5/_8$" wide. From these strips, cut 11 strips (**H**) $1^5/_8$" x 20" for strip sets.

From binding fabric:
- Cut 11 strips $2^1/_2$" wide.

MAKING THE BLOCKS

Paper Piecing the Block

*Photocopy the **Paper Piecing Pattern**, page 12, at 162%.*

1. To make four patch block for area 1 of pattern, follow **Piecing** and **Pressing**, page 32, to sew 1 blue print strip (**G**) and 1 floral print strip (**H**) together as shown to make **Strip Set**. Make 11 **Strip Sets**. Cut across **Strip Sets** at $1^5/_8$" intervals to make **Unit 1**. Make 128 **Unit 1's**.

Strip Set
(make 11)

Unit 1
(make 128)

2. Sew 2 Unit 1's together as shown to make **Unit 2**. Make 64 **Unit 2's**.

Unit 2
(make 64)

3. On the back side of the foundation pattern, completely cover area 1 with a **Unit 2**. (The right side of the fabric will be facing up.) Pin or glue fabric in place making sure **Unit 2** is centered on the foundaton (**Fig. 1**). Fold foundation on line between area 1 and area 2. Trim fabric $1/_4$" from fold (**Fig. 2**). Unfold foundation.

Fig. 1

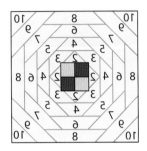

Fig. 2

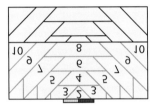

4. Matching trimmed edges, place a No. 2 white print rectangle on **Unit 2**, right sides together, making sure fabric extends beyond outer edges of area 2. Turn foundation over to front and pin. Sew along line between areas 1 and 2, extending sewing a few stitches beyond beginning and end of line (**Fig. 3**).

Fig. 3

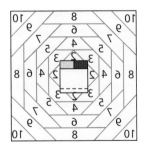

5. Open out rectangle; press. Pin rectangle to foundation (**Fig. 4**).

Fig. 4

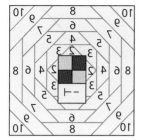

6. Continue adding pieces in the same manner in numerical order until foundation is covered. Cover areas 2, 4, 6, and 8 using the white print. Alternating the blue print and the floral print, cover areas 3, 5, 7, and 9. Cover 2 area 10's using the rose print and 2 using the floral print. Trim fabric and foundation ¼" from outer edges to make **Block**. Make 64 **Blocks**.

Block Diagram
(make 64)

ASSEMBLING THE QUILT TOP

*Follow **Piecing** and **Pressing**, page 32, to make the quilt top. Refer to photo, page 9, and **Quilt Top Diagram**, page 13, for placement.*

1. Sew 8 **Blocks** together as shown to make a **Row**. Make 8 **Rows**.
2. Sew **Rows** together to make **Quilt Top Center**.

ADDING THE BORDERS

For all borders, match centers and corners and ease in fullness.

1. Sew rose print inner side borders (**A**), then rose print inner top/bottom borders (**B**) to **Quilt Top Center**.
2. Sew white print middle side borders (**C**), then white print middle top/bottom borders (**D**) to pieced center.
3. Sew blue print outer side borders (**E**), then blue print outer top/bottom borders (**F**) to pieced center to make quilt top.

COMPLETING THE QUILT

1. Follow **Quilting**, page 34, to mark, layer, and quilt as desired. Our quilt was machine quilted.
2. Follow **Making Straight-Grain Binding**, page 37, to make 11⅝ yds of 2½"w binding.
3. Follow **Attaching Binding with Mitered Corners**, page 37, to attach binding to quilt.

Paper Piecing Pattern

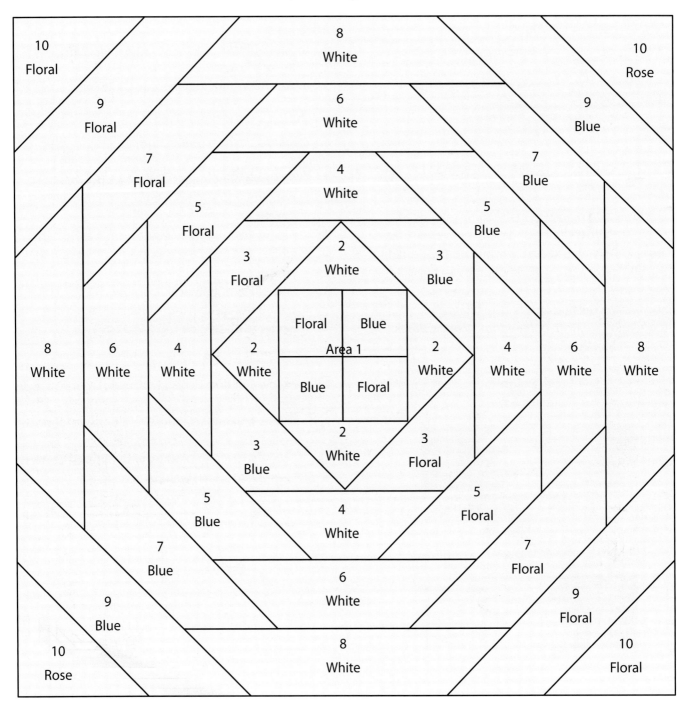

Note: Photocopy pattern at 162%.

Simple Circles

It's oh-so simple to evoke
the magical wonder of
a swirling kaleidoscope,
thanks to fool-the-
eye circle appliqués.
This rainbow of colors
enchants the eyes, while
fanciful buttons accent
the playful mood.

Pieced by Patty Hawkins.
Finished Block Size: 11" x 11" (28 cm x 28 cm)
Finished Quilt Size: 58" x 69" (147 cm x 175 cm)

YARDAGE REQUIREMENTS

Yardage is based on 43"/44" (109 cm/112 cm) wide fabric with a usable width of 40" (102 cm).

$\frac{1}{4}$ yd (23 cm) ***each*** of 20 assorted light and 20 assorted dark print fabrics

$1\frac{3}{4}$ yds (1.6 m) of dark green print fabric for inner borders

$1\frac{1}{8}$ yds (1.7 m) of green print fabric for outer borders

$4\frac{3}{8}$ yds (4.0 m) of backing fabric

$\frac{5}{8}$ yd (57 cm) of binding fabric

66" x 77" (168 cm x 196 cm) piece of batting

You will also need:

Paper-backed fusible web

Stabilizer

Eighty assorted 1" diameter (25 mm) buttons

CUTTING OUT THE PIECES

Measurements for squares and borders include $\frac{1}{4}$" seam allowances. Appliqué pattern, page 16, does not include seam allowances. Follow Rotary Cutting, page 31, to cut fabric. Cutting lengths given for borders are exact.

From each light and dark print fabric:

- Cut 1 strip 6" wide. From this strip, cut 2 squares (**A**) 6" x 6".

From ***each*** remaining width:

- Follow **Preparing Fusible Appliqué Pieces**, page 33, and use pattern, page 16, to cut 8 quarter-circles (**B**).

From dark green print fabric:

- Cut 2 *lengthwise* inner side borders (**C**) 2" x $55\frac{1}{2}$".
- Cut 2 *lengthwise* inner top/bottom borders (**D**) 2" x $47\frac{1}{2}$".

From green print fabric:

- Cut 2 *lengthwise* outer side borders (**E**) $5\frac{1}{2}$" x $58\frac{1}{2}$".
- Cut 2 *lengthwise* outer top/bottom borders (**F**) $5\frac{1}{2}$" x $57\frac{1}{2}$".

From binding fabric:

- Cut 7 strips $2\frac{1}{2}$" wide.

MAKING THE BLOCKS

*Follow **Piecing** and **Pressing**, page 32, and **Preparing Fusible Appliqué Pieces**, page 33, to make blocks. Refer to **Block Diagram** and photo, page 15, for placement. **Note:** We used a machine Blanket Stitch to attach appliqués. You may also appliqué them using 2 strands of embroidery floss and a hand Blanket Stitch.*

1. Matching corners and edges, position 4 like light print quarter-circles (**B**) on 1 dark print square (**A**) and fuse in place. Follow **Decorative Stitch Appliqué**, page 33, to appliqué quarter-circles using black thread and a machine Blanket Stitch. Make 40 **Unit 1's** (2 each of like prints).

Unit 1
(make 40)

2. Using the same 2 prints in reverse [4 like dark print quarter-circles (**B**) and 1 light print square (**A**)], repeat Step 1 to make **Unit 2**. Make 40 **Unit 2's** (2 each of like prints).

Unit 2
(make 40)

3. Sew 2 **Unit 1's** and 2 **Unit 2's** of the same prints together as shown to make **Block**. Make 20 **Blocks**.

Block Diagram
(make 20)

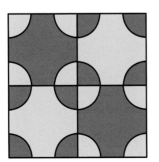

ASSEMBLING THE QUILT TOP

*Refer to **Quilt Top Diagram** for placement.*

1. Sew 4 **Blocks** together to make a **Row**. Make 5 **Rows**.
2. Sew **Rows** together to make **Quilt Top Center**.

ADDING THE BORDERS

For all borders, match centers and corners and ease in fullness.

1. Sew inner side borders (**C**), then inner top/bottom borders (**D**) to **Quilt Top Center**.
2. Sew outer side borders (**E**), then outer top/bottom borders (**F**) to pieced center to make quilt top.

COMPLETING THE QUILT

1. Follow **Quilting**, page 34, to mark, layer, and quilt as desired. Our quilt was machine quilted.
2. Follow **Making Straight-Grain Binding**, page 37, to make 7^1/$_2$ yds of 2^1/$_2$"w binding.
3. Follow **Attaching Binding with Mitered Corners**, page 37, to attach binding to quilt.
4. Referring to photo for placement, sew a button in the center of each square.

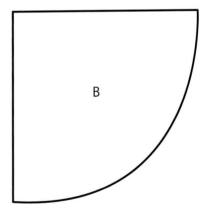

Quilt Top Diagram

Double Irish Chain

Crimson and sage prints give a classic design a dramatic new look. This creative take on the beloved Double Irish Chain pattern is both strikingly stylish and comfortingly familiar.

Pieced by Patty Hawkins.
Finished Block Size: 10" x 10" (25 cm x 25 cm)
Finished Quilt Size: 85" x 105" (216 cm x 267 cm)

YARDAGE REQUIREMENTS

Yardage is based on 43"/44" (109 cm/112 cm) wide fabric with a usable width of 40" (102 cm).

- 2³/₄ yds (2.5 m) of red print fabric
- 4¹/₂ yds (4.1 m) of green print fabric
- 3¹/₂ yds (3.2 m) of beige print fabric
- 7³/₄ yds (7.1 m) of backing fabric
- ⁷/₈ yd (80 cm) of binding fabric
- 93" x 113" (236 cm x 287 cm) piece of batting

CUTTING OUT THE PIECES

*All measurements include ¹/₄" seam allowances. Follow **Rotary Cutting**, page 31, to cut fabric. Cutting lengths given for borders are exact.*

From red print fabric:
- Cut 2 *lengthwise* inner side borders (**A**) 2¹/₂" x 90¹/₂".
- Cut 2 *lengthwise* inner top/bottom borders (**B**) 2¹/₂" x 74¹/₂".

From remaining width:
- Cut 36 strips (**C**) 2¹/₂" x 21".

From green print fabric:
- Cut 3 strips 21" wide. From these strips, cut 48 *lengthwise* strips (**F**) 2¹/₂" x 21".
- Cut 2 *lengthwise* outer side borders (**D**) 5¹/₂" x 94¹/₂".
- Cut 2 *lengthwise* outer top/bottom borders (**E**) 5¹/₂" x 84¹/₂".

From remaining width:
- Cut 3 strips 21" wide. From these strips, cut 16 *lengthwise* strips (**F**) 2¹/₂" x 21".

From beige print fabric:
- Cut 4 strips 6¹/₂" wide. From these strips, cut 19 squares (**I**) 6¹/₂" x 6¹/₂".
- Cut 11 strips 2¹/₂" wide. From these strips, cut 62 rectangles (**J**) 2¹/₂" x 6¹/₂".
- Cut 2 strips 21" wide. From these strips, cut 16 *lengthwise* strips (**G**) 2¹/₂" x 21" and 6 *lengthwise* strips (**H**) 6¹/₂" x 21".

- Cut 1 strip 21" wide. From this strip, cut 2 *lengthwise* strips (**H**) 6½" x 21".

From remaining width:
- Cut 3 *crosswise* strips 6½" wide. From these strips, cut 12 squares (**I**) 6½" x 6½".

From binding fabric:
- Cut 11 strips 2½" wide.

MAKING THE BLOCKS

*Follow **Piecing and Pressing**, page 32, to make the blocks.*

Block A

1. Sew 2 red print strips (**C**), 2 green print strips (**F**), and 1 beige print strip (**G**) together as shown to make **Strip Set A**. Make 8 **Strip Set A's**. Cut across **Strip Set A's** at 2½" intervals to make **Unit 1**. Make 64 **Unit 1's**.

Strip Set A
(make 8)

Unit 1
(make 64)

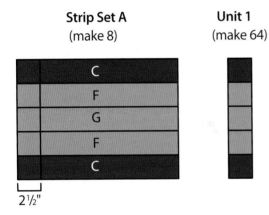

2. Sew 2 red print strips (**C**) and 3 green print strips (**F**) together as shown to make **Strip Set B**. Make 8 **Strip Set B's**. Cut across **Strip Set B's** at 2½" intervals to make **Unit 2**. Make 64 **Unit 2's**.

Strip Set B
(make 8)

Unit 2
(make 64)

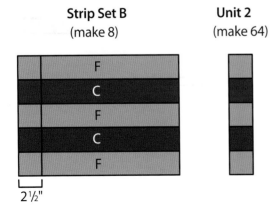

3. Sew 1 red print strip (**C**), 2 green print strips (**F**), and 2 beige print strips (**G**) together as shown to make **Strip Set C**. Make 4 **Strip Set C's**. Cut across **Strip Set C's** at 2½" intervals to make **Unit 3**. Make 32 **Unit 3's**.

Strip Set C
(make 4)

Unit 3
(make 32)

4. Sew 2 **Unit 1's**, 2 **Unit 2's**, and 1 **Unit 3** together as shown to make **Block A**. Make 32 **Block A's**.

Block A Diagram
(make 32)

5. (no text)

Block B

1. Sew 2 green print strips (**F**) and 1 beige print strip (**H**) together as shown to make **Strip Set D**. Make 8 **Strip Set D's**. Cut across **Strip Set D's** at 2½" intervals to make **Unit 4**. Make 62 **Unit 4's**.

Strip Set D
(make 8)

Unit 4
(make 62)

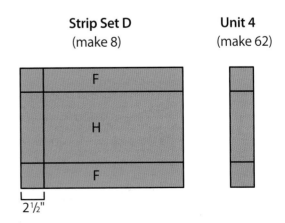

2. Sew 2 beige print rectangles (**J**), 2 **Unit 4's**, and 1 beige print square (**I**) together as shown to make **Block B**. Make 31 **Block B's**.

Block B Diagram
(make 31)

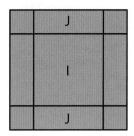

ASSEMBLING THE QUILT TOP
Refer to Quilt Top Diagram for placement.

1. Sew 4 **Block A's** and 3 **Block B's** together to make **Row A**. Make 5 **Row A's**.
2. Sew 3 **Block A's** and 4 **Block B's** together to make **Row B**. Make 4 **Row B's**.
3. Sew **Rows A** and **B** together to make **Quilt Top Center**.

ADDING THE BORDERS
For all borders, match centers and corners and ease in fullness.

1. Sew red print inner side borders (**A**), then red print inner top/ bottom borders (**B**) to **Quilt Top Center**.
2. Sew green print outer side borders (**D**), then green print outer top/ bottom borders (**E**) to pieced center to make quilt top.

COMPLETING THE QUILT

1. Follow **Quilting**, page 34, to mark, layer, and quilt as desired. Our quilt was machine quilted.
2. Follow **Making Straight-Grain Binding**, page 37, to make 11 yds of 2$\frac{1}{2}$"w binding.
3. Follow **Attaching Binding with Mitered Corners**, page 37, to attach binding to quilt.

Quilt Top Diagram

Remember When

Bring back fond memories of younger years with a nostalgic cover-up. Dark triangles are the perfect complement to a whimsical children's print, giving playtime a grown-up appeal.

Pieced by Patty Hawkins.
Finished Block Size: 8" x 8" (20 cm x 20 cm)
Finished Quilt Size: 61" x 69" (155 cm x 175 cm)

YARDAGE REQUIREMENTS

Yardage is based on 43"/44" (109 cm/112 cm) wide fabric with a usable width of 40" (102 cm).

- 2³/₄ yds (2.5 m) of cream print fabric
- 1¹/₈ yds (1.0 m) total of assorted dark print fabrics
- 1¹/₂ yds (1.4 m) of khaki print fabric for inner borders
- ³/₈ yd (34 cm) of red print fabric for corner squares
- 4³/₈ yds (4.0 m) of backing fabric
- ⁵/₈ yd (57 cm) of binding fabric
- 69" x 77" (175 cm x 196 cm) piece of batting

CUTTING OUT THE PIECES

*All measurements include ¹/₄" seam allowances. Follow **Rotary Cutting**, page 31, to cut fabric. Cutting lengths given for borders are exact.*

From cream print fabric:
- Cut 4 strips 8⁷/₈" wide. From these strips, cut 15 squares (**A**) 8⁷/₈" x 8⁷/₈".
- Cut 2 *lengthwise* outer side borders (**B**) 8¹/₂" x 52¹/₂".
- Cut 2 *lengthwise* outer top/bottom borders (**C**) 8¹/₂" x 44¹/₂".

From assorted dark print fabrics:
- Cut 15 squares (**D**) 8⁷/₈" x 8⁷/₈".

From khaki print fabric:
- Cut 2 *lengthwise* inner side borders (**E**) 2¹/₂" x 48¹/₂".
- Cut 2 *lengthwise* inner top/bottom borders (**F**) 2¹/₂" x 44¹/₂".

From red print fabric:
- Cut 1 strip 8¹/₂" wide. From this strip, cut 4 corner squares (**G**) 8¹/₂" x 8¹/₂".

From binding fabric:
- Cut 7 strips 2¹/₂" wide.

MAKING THE BLOCKS

*Follow **Piecing** and **Pressing**, page 32, to make the blocks.*

1. Draw a diagonal line (corner to corner) on wrong side of each cream print square (**A**). With right sides together, place a cream print square (**A**) on top of a dark print square (**D**). Stitch seam ¹/₄" from each side of drawn line (**Fig. 1**).

Fig. 1

2. Trim along drawn line and press open to make 2 **Blocks**. Make 30 **Blocks**.

Block Diagram
(make 30)

ASSEMBLING THE QUILT TOP

*Refer to photo, page 23, and **Quilt Top Diagram** for placement.*

1. Sew 5 **Blocks** together as shown to make a **Row**. Make 6 **Rows**.
2. Sew 6 **Rows** together as shown to make **Quilt Top Center**.

ADDING THE BORDERS

For all borders, match centers and corners and ease in fullness.

1. Sew inner side borders (**E**), then inner top/bottom borders (**F**) to **Quilt Top Center**.
2. Sew outer side borders (**B**) to pieced center.
3. Sew 1 corner square (**G**) to each end of top and bottom borders (**C**) to make 2 **Border Units**.
4. Sew a **Border Unit** to the top and bottom of pieced center to make quilt top.

COMPLETING THE QUILT

1. Follow **Quilting**, page 34, to mark, layer, and quilt as desired. Our quilt was machine quilted.
2. Follow **Making Straight-Grain Binding**, page 37, to make 7⅝ yds of 2¹/₂"w binding.
3. Follow **Attaching Binding with Mitered Corners**, page 37, to attach binding to quilt.

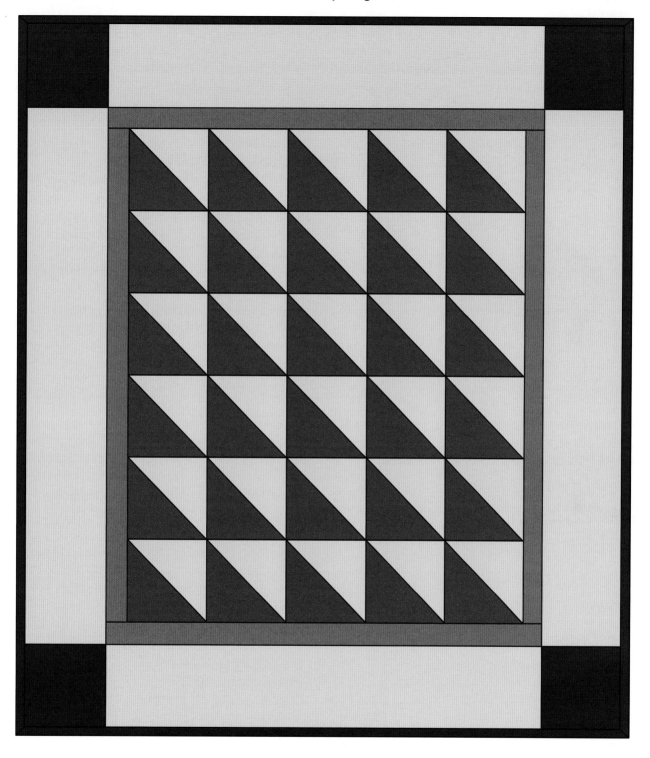

Church in the Wildwood

Lush autumn colors and appliquéd leaves make this striking quilt just right for a brisk fall afternoon. And if you look closely, a hidden country church is just waiting to be discovered.

Finished Block Size: 10¹/₂" x 10¹/₂" (27 cm x 27 cm)
Finished Quilt Size: 72" x 82¹/₂" (183 cm x 210 cm)

YARDAGE REQUIREMENTS

Yardage is based on 43"/44" (109 cm/112 cm) wide fabric with a usable width of 40" (102 cm).

¹/₄ yd (23 cm) of red print fabric for block centers

6 yds (5.5 m) **total** of assorted print fabrics for blocks and appliqués

2¹/₂ yds (2.3 m) of gold print fabric for borders

6³/₄ yds (6.2 m) of backing fabric

³/₄ yd (69 cm) of binding fabric

80" x 91" (203 cm x 231 cm) piece of batting

You will also need:

Paper-backed fusible web

Stabilizer

CUTTING OUT THE PIECES

*Measurements for Log Cabin Block pieces and borders include ¹/₄" seam allowances. Follow **Rotary Cutting**, page 31, to cut fabric. Cutting lengths given for borders are exact. Appliqué patterns, page 30, are reversed. Follow **Preparing Fusible Appliqué Pieces**, page 33, to cut out appliqués.*

From red print fabric:

- Cut 3 strips 2" wide. From these strips, cut 42 squares (**A**) 2" x 2".

From assorted print fabrics for Log Cabin Blocks:

- Cut 42 squares (**B**) 2" x 2".
- Cut 84 rectangles (**C**) 2" x 3¹/₂".
- Cut 84 rectangles (**D**) 2" x 5".
- Cut 84 rectangles (**E**) 2" x 6¹/₂".
- Cut 84 rectangles (**F**) 2" x 8".
- Cut 84 rectangles (**G**) 2" x 9¹/₂".
- Cut 42 rectangles (**H**) 2" x 11".

From assorted print fabrics for appliques:

- Use patterns, page 30, to cut 32 assorted leaves (some patterns may be reversed for variety, if desired).

From gold print fabric:

- Cut 2 *lengthwise* top/bottom borders (**I**) 4¹/₂" x 63¹/₂".
- Cut 2 *lengthwise* side borders (**J**) 4¹/₂" x 82".

From binding fabric:

- Cut 9 strips 2¹/₂" wide.

MAKING THE BLOCKS

*Follow **Piecing** and **Pressing**, page 32, to make blocks. Refer to **Block Diagram** and **Quilt Top Diagram** for placement.*

1. Sew 1 red print square (**A**) and 1 print square (**B**) together as shown to make **Unit 1**. Make 42 **Unit 1's**.

Unit 1
(make 42)

2. Sew 1 print rectangle (**C**) and **Unit 1** together as shown to make **Unit 2**. Make 42 **Unit 2's**.

Unit 2
(make 42)

3. Sew a 2nd print rectangle (**C**) and **Unit 2** together as shown to make **Unit 3**. Make 42 **Unit 3's**.

Unit 3
(make 42)

4. Continue adding print rectangles (**D-H**) in alphabetical order as shown to make **Log Cabin Block**. Make 42 **Log Cabin Blocks**.

Log Cabin Block Diagram
(make 42)

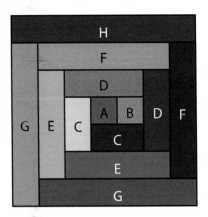

ASSEMBLING THE QUILT TOP

*Refer to photo, page 27, and **Quilt Top Diagram** for placement.*

1. Sew 6 **Log Cabin Blocks** together to make a **Row**. Make 7 **Rows**.
2. Sew **Rows** together to make **Quilt Top Center**.
3. Matching centers and corners and easing in fullness, sew top/bottom borders (**I**), then side borders (**J**) to **Quilt Top Center**.
4. Position leaves as desired on quilt top and fuse in place. Follow **Decorative Stitch Appliqué**, page 33, to appliqué leaves using ecru thread and a machine Blanket Stitch.

COMPLETING THE QUILT

1. Follow **Quilting**, page 34, to mark, layer, and quilt as desired. Our quilt was machine quilted.
2. Follow **Making Straight-Grain Binding**, page 37, to make 9 yds of 2¹/₂"w binding.
3. Follow **Attaching Binding with Mitered Corners**, page 37, to attach binding to quilt.

Quilt Top Diagram

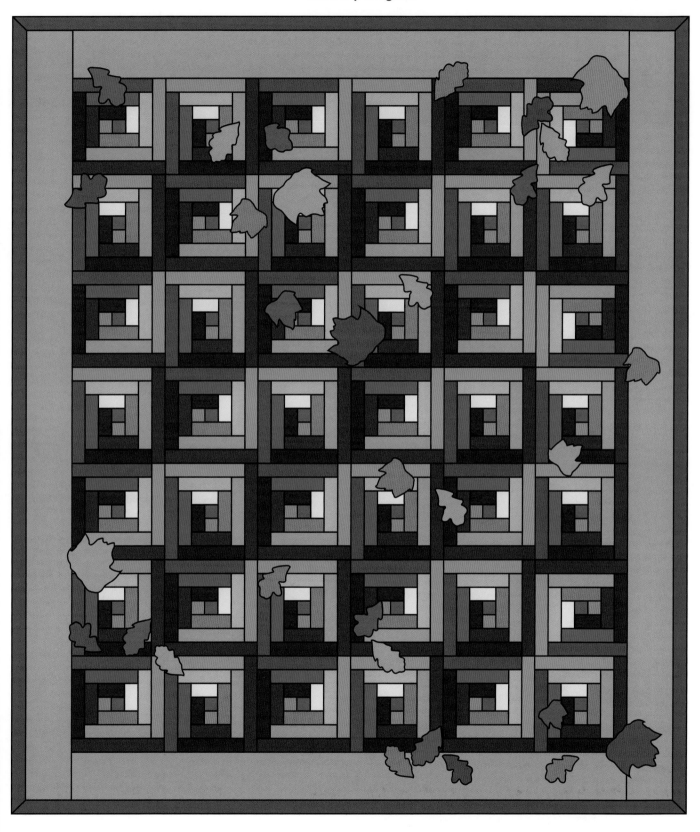

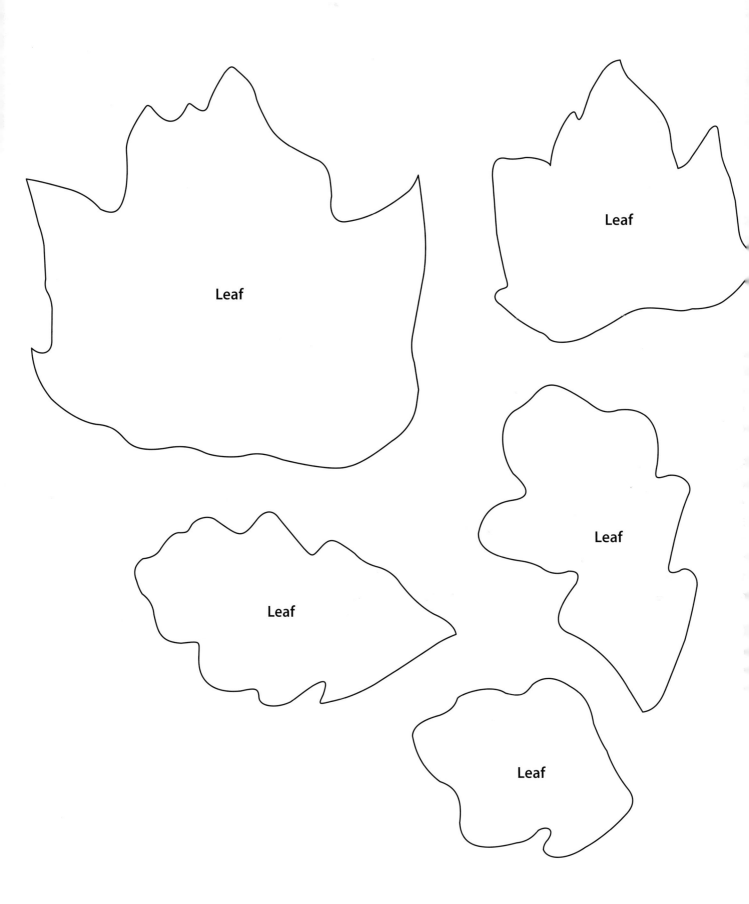

Leaf

Leaf

Leaf

Leaf

Leaf

General Instructions

To make your quilting easier and more enjoyable, we encourage you to carefully read all of the general instructions, study the color photographs, and familiarize yourself with the individual project instructions before beginning a project.

FABRICS

SELECTING FABRICS

Choose high-quality, medium-weight 100% cotton fabrics. All-cotton fabrics hold a crease better, fray less, and are easier to quilt than cotton/polyester blends.

Yardage requirements listed for each project are based on 43"/44" wide fabric with a "usable" width of 40" after shrinkage and trimming selvages. Actual usable width will probably vary slightly from fabric to fabric. Our recommended yardage lengths should be adequate for occasional re-squaring of fabric when many cuts are required.

PREPARING FABRICS

We recommend that all fabrics be washed, dried, and pressed before cutting. If fabrics are not pre-washed, washing finished quilt will cause shrinkage and give it a more "antiqued" look and feel. Bright and dark colors, which may run, should always be washed before cutting. After washing and drying fabric, fold lengthwise with wrong sides together and matching selvages.

ROTARY CUTTING

Rotary cutting has brought speed and accuracy to quiltmaking by allowing quilters to easily cut strips of fabric and then cut those strips into smaller pieces.

Place fabric on work surface with fold closest to you.

Cut all strips from selvage-to-selvage width of fabric unless otherwise indicated in project instructions.

Square left edge of fabric using rotary cutter and rulers (**Figs. 1-2**).

Fig. 1

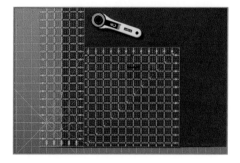

Fig. 2

- To cut each strip required for a project, place ruler over cut edge of fabric, aligning desired marking on ruler with cut edge; make cut (**Fig. 3**).

Fig. 3

- When cutting several strips from a single piece of fabric, it is important to make sure that cuts remain at a perfect right angle to the fold; square fabric as needed.

PIECING

Precise cutting, followed by accurate piecing, will ensure that all pieces of quilt top fit together well.

MACHINE PIECING

- Set sewing machine stitch length for approximately 11 stitches per inch.
- Use neutral-colored general-purpose sewing thread (not quilting thread) in needle and in bobbin.
- An accurate $1/4$" seam allowance is *essential*. Presser feet that are $1/4$" wide are available for most sewing machines.
- When piecing, always place pieces right sides together and match raw edges; pin if necessary.
- Chain piecing saves time and will usually result in more accurate piecing.
- Trim away points of seam allowances that extend beyond edges of sewn pieces.

SEWING STRIP SETS

When there are several strips to assemble into a strip set, first sew strips together into pairs, then sew pairs together to form strip set. To help avoid distortion, sew seams in opposite directions (**Fig. 4**).

Fig. 4

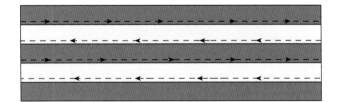

SEWING ACROSS SEAM INTERSECTIONS

When sewing across intersection of 2 seams, place pieces right sides together and match seams exactly, making sure seam allowances are pressed in opposite directions (**Fig. 5**)

Fig. 5

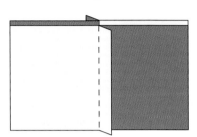

PRESSING

- Use steam iron set on "Cotton" for all pressing.
- Press after sewing each seam.
- Seam allowances are almost always pressed to 1 side, usually toward darker fabric. However, to reduce bulk it may occasionally be necessary to press seam allowances toward the lighter fabric or even to press them open.
- To prevent dark fabric seam allowance from showing through light fabric, trim darker seam allowance slightly narrower than lighter seam allowance.
- To press long seams, such as those in long strip sets, without curving or other distortion, lay strips across width of the ironing board.

MACHINE APPLIQUÉ

PREPARING APPLIQUÉ PIECES

White or light-colored fabrics may need to be lined with fusible interfacing before applying fusible web to prevent darker fabrics from showing through.

- Place paper-backed fusible web, paper side up, over appliqué pattern. Trace pattern onto paper side of web with pencil as many times as indicated in project instructions for a single fabric. Follow manufacturer's instructions to fuse traced patterns to wrong side of fabrics. Do not remove paper backing.
- Use scissors to cut out appliqué pieces along traced lines. Remove paper backing from all pieces.

DECORATIVE STITCH APPLIQUÉ

Some sewing machines feature a Blanket Stitch similar to the one used in this book. Refer to your Owner's Manual for machine set-up. If your machine does not have this stitch, try any of the decorative stitches your machine has until you are satisfied with the look.

- Thread sewing machine and bobbin with general-purpose thread.
- Attach an open-toe presser foot. Select far right needle position and needle down (if your machine has these features).
- Pin a stabilizer, such as paper or any of the commercially available products, on wrong side of background fabric before stitching appliqués in place.
- Position quilt top under presser foot where you will begin stitching. Bring bobbin thread to the top of the fabric by lowering then raising the needle, bringing up the bobbin thread loop. Pull the loop all the way to the surface.
- Begin by stitching 5 or 6 stitches in place (drop feed dogs or set stitch length at 0), or use your machine's lock stitch feature, if equipped, to anchor thread. Return setting to selected Blanket Stitch.
- Most of the Blanket Stitch should be done on the appliqué with the right edges of the stitch falling at the very outside edge of the appliqué. Stitch over all exposed raw edges of the appliqué pieces.

7. (*Note:* Dots on **Figs. 6-11** indicate where to leave the needle in the fabric when pivoting.) Always stopping with the needle down in the background fabric, refer to **Fig. 6** to stitch outside points like tips of leaves. Stop one stitch short of point. Raise presser foot. Pivot project slightly, lower presser foot, and make one angled Stitch 1. Take next stitch, stop at point, and pivot so Stitch 2 will be perpendicular to point. Pivot slightly to make Stitch 3. Continue stitching.

Fig. 6

8. For outside corners (**Fig. 7**), stitch to the corner, stopping with needle in background fabric. Raise presser foot. Pivot project, lower presser foot, and take an angled stitch. Raise presser foot. Pivot project, lower presser foot and stitch adjacent side.

Fig. 7

9. For inside corners (**Fig. 8**), stitch to the corner, taking the last bite at corner and stopping with the needle down in background fabric. Raise presser foot. Pivot project, lower presser foot, and take an angled stitch. Raise presser foot. Pivot projects, lower presser foot and stitch adjacent side.

Fig. 8

10. When stitching outside curves (**Fig. 9**), stop with needle down in background fabric. Raise presser foot and pivot project as needed. Lower presser foot and continue stitching, pivoting as often as necessary to follow curve. Small circles may require pivoting between each stitch.

Fig. 9

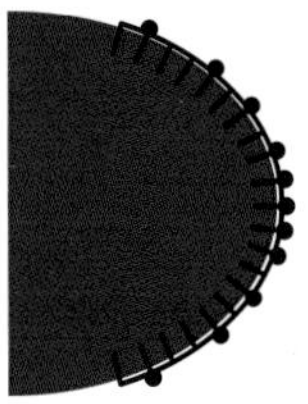

11. When stitching inside curves (**Fig. 10**), stop with the needle down in background fabric. Raise presser foot and pivot project as needed. Lower presser foot and continue stitching, pivoting as often as necessary to follow curve.

Fig. 10

12. When stopping stitching, use a lock stitch to sew 5 or 6 stitches in place or use a needle to pull threads to wrong side of background fabric (**Fig. 11**); knot, then trim ends.

Fig. 11

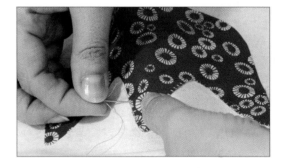

QUILTING

*Quilting holds the 3 layers (top, batting, and backing) of the quilt together and can be done by hand or machine. Because marking, layering, and quilting are interrelated and may be done in different orders depending on circumstances, please read entire **Quilting** section before beginning project.*

TYPES OF QUILTING DESIGNS
In the Ditch Quilting
Quilting along seamlines or along edges of appliquéd piec is called "in the ditch" quilting. This type of quilting should done on side opposite seam allowance and does not have be marked.

Outline Quilting

Quilting a consistent distance, usually $1/4$", from seam or appliqué is called "outline" quilting. Outline quilting may be marked, or $1/4$" masking tape may be placed along seamlines or quilting guide. (Do not leave tape on quilt longer than necessary, since it may leave an adhesive residue.)

Motif Quilting

Quilting a design, such as a feathered wreath, is called "motif" quilting. This type of quilting should be marked before basting quilt layers together.

Echo Quilting

Quilting that follows the outline of an appliquéd or pieced design with 2 or more parallel lines is called "echo" quilting. This type of quilting does not need to be marked.

Meandering Quilting

Quilting in random curved lines and swirls is called "meandering" quilting. Quilting lines should not cross or touch each other. This type of quilting does not need to be marked.

Stipple Quilting

Meandering quilting that is very closely spaced is called "stipple" quilting. Stippling will flatten the area quilted and is often stitched in background areas to raise appliquéd or pieced designs. This type of quilting does not need to be marked.

MARKING QUILTING LINES

Quilting lines may be marked using fabric marking pencils, chalk markers, water- or air-soluble pens, or lead pencils.

Simple quilting designs may be marked with chalk or chalk pencil after basting. A small area may be marked, then quilted, before moving to next area to be marked. Intricate designs should be marked before basting using a more durable marker.

Caution: Some marks may be permanently set by pressing. **Test** different markers **on scrap fabric** to find one that marks clearly and can be thoroughly removed.

A wide variety of precut quilting stencils, as well as entire books of quilting patterns, are available. Using a stencil makes it easier to mark intricate or repetitive designs.

To make a stencil from a pattern, center template plastic over pattern and use a permanent marker to trace pattern onto plastic. Use a craft knife with single or double blade to cut channels along traced lines (**Fig. 12**).

Fig. 12

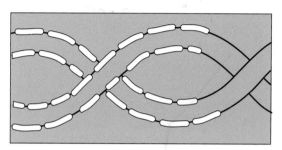

PREPARING THE BACKING

To allow for slight shifting of quilt top during quilting, backing should be approximately 4" larger on all sides. Yardage requirements listed for quilt backings are calculated for 43"/44"w fabric. Using 90"w or 108"w fabric for the backing of a bed-sized quilt may eliminate piecing. To piece a backing using 43"/44"w fabric, use the following instructions.

1. Measure length and width of quilt top; add 8" to each measurement.
2. If determined width is 79" or less, cut backing fabric into 2 lengths slightly longer than determined length measurement. Trim selvages. Place lengths with right sides facing and sew long edges together, forming tube (**Fig. 13**). Match seams and press along 1 fold (**Fig. 14**). Cut along pressed fold to form single piece (**Fig. 15**).

Fig. 13	**Fig. 14**	**Fig. 15**

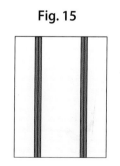

3. If determined width is more than 79", cut backing fabric into 3 lengths slightly longer than determined **width** measurement. Trim selvages. Sew long edges together to form single piece.

4. Trim backing to size determined in Step 1; press seam allowances open.

CHOOSING THE BATTING

The appropriate batting will make quilting easier. For fine hand quilting, choose low-loft batting. All cotton or cotton/polyester blend battings work well for machine quilting because the cotton helps "grip" quilt layers. If quilt is to be tied, a high-loft batting, sometimes called extra-loft or fat batting, may be used to make quilt "fluffy."

Types of batting include cotton, polyester, cotton/polyester blend, wool, cotton/wool blend, and silk.

When selecting batting, refer to package labels for characteristics and care instructions. Cut batting same size as prepared backing.

ASSEMBLING THE QUILT

1. Examine wrong side of quilt top closely; trim any seam allowances and clip any threads that may show through front of the quilt. Press quilt top, being careful not to "set" any marked quilting lines.

2. Place backing **wrong** side up on flat surface. Use masking tape to tape edges of backing to surface. Place batting on top of backing fabric. Smooth batting gently, being careful not to stretch or tear. Center quilt top **right** side up on batting.

3. Use 1" rustproof safety pins to "pin-baste" all layers together, spacing pins approximately 4" apart. Begin at center and work toward outer edges to secure all layers. If possible, place pins away from areas that will be quilted, although pins may be removed as needed when quilting.

MACHINE QUILTING METHODS

Use general-purpose thread in bobbin. Do not use quilting thread. Thread the needle of machine with general-purpose thread or transparent monofilament thread to make quilting blend with quilt top fabrics. Use decorative thread, such as a metallic or contrasting-color general-purpose thread, to make quilting lines stand out more.

Straight Line Quilting

The term "straight-line" is somewhat deceptive, since curves (especially gentle ones) as well as straight lines can be stitched with this technique.

1. Set stitch length for 6 - 10 stitches per inch and attach walking foot to sewing machine.

2. Determine which section of quilt will have the longest continuous quilting line, oftentimes the area from center top to center bottom. Roll up and secure each edge of quilt to help reduce the bulk, keeping fabrics smooth. Smaller projects may not need to be rolled.

3. Begin stitching on longest quilting line, using very short stitches for the first $1/4$" to "lock" quilting. Stitch across project, using 1 hand on each side of walking foot to slightly spread fabric and to guide fabric through machine. Lock stitches at end of quilting line.

4. Continue machine quilting, stitching longer quilting lines first to stabilize quilt before moving on to other areas.

Free Motion Quilting

Free motion quilting may be free form or may follow a marked pattern.

1. Attach darning foot to sewing machine and lower or cover feed dogs.
2. Position quilt under darning foot. Holding top thread, take 1 stitch and pull bobbin thread to top of quilt. To "lock" beginning of quilting line, hold top and bobbin threads while making 3 to 5 stitches in place.
3. Use 1 hand on each side of darning foot to slightly spread fabric and to move fabric through the machine. Even stitch length is achieved by using smooth, flowing hand motion and steady machine speed. Slow machine speed and fast hand movement will create long stitches. Fast machine speed and slow hand movement will create short stitches. Move quilt sideways, back and forth, in a circular motion, or in a random motion to create desired designs; do not rotate quilt. Lock stitches at end of each quilting line.

BINDING

Binding encloses the raw edges of quilt. Because of its stretchiness, bias binding works well for binding projects with curves or rounded corners and tends to lie smooth and flat in any given circumstance. Binding may also be cut from straight lengthwise or crosswise grain of fabric.

MAKING STRAIGHT-GRAIN BINDING

. Cut lengthwise or crosswise strips of binding fabric the determined length and the width called for in project instructions. Piece strips to achieve necessary length.
. Matching wrong sides and raw edges, press strip(s) in half lengthwise to complete binding.

ATTACHING BINDING WITH MITERED CORNERS

. Beginning with 1 end near center on bottom edge of quilt, lay binding around quilt to make sure that seams in binding will not end up at a corner. Adjust placement if necessary. Matching raw edges of binding to raw edge of quilt top, pin binding to right side of quilt along 1 edge.
. When you reach first corner, mark ¼" from corner of quilt top (**Fig. 16**).

Fig. 16

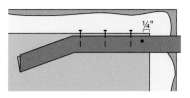

3. Beginning approximately 10" from end of binding and using ¼" seam allowance, sew binding to quilt, backstitching at beginning of stitching and at mark (**Fig. 17**). Lift needle out of fabric and clip thread.

Fig. 17

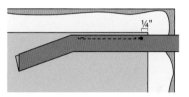

4. Fold binding as shown in **Figs. 18–19** and pin binding to adjacent side, matching raw edges. When reaching the next corner, mark ¼" from edge of quilt top.

Fig. 18   **Fig. 19**

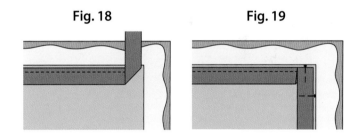

5. Backstitching at edge of quilt top, sew pinned binding to quilt (**Fig. 20**); backstitch at the next mark. Lift needle out of fabric and clip thread.

Fig. 20

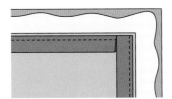

6. Continue sewing binding to quilt, stopping approximately 10" from starting point (**Fig. 21**).

Fig. 21

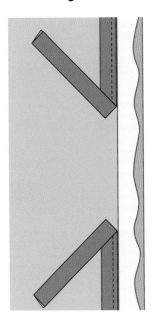

7. Bring beginning and end of binding to center of opening and fold each end back, leaving a $^1/_4$" space between folds (**Fig. 22**). Finger-press folds.

Fig. 22

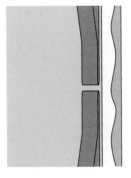

8. Unfold ends of binding and draw a line across wrong side in finger-pressed crease. Draw a line through the lengthwise pressed fold of binding at same spot to create a cross mark. With edge of ruler at marked cross, line up 45° angle marking on ruler with one long side of binding. Draw a diagonal line from edge to edge. Repeat on remaining end, making sure that the two lines are angled the same way (**Fig. 23**).

Fig. 23

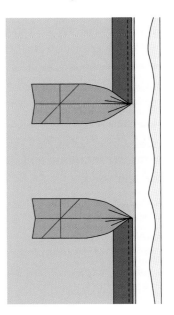

9. Matching right sides and diagonal lines, pin binding ends together at right angles (**Fig. 24**).

Fig. 24

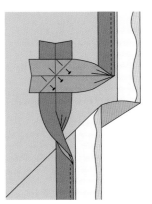

10. Machine stitch along diagonal line, removing pins as you stitch (**Fig. 25**).

Fig. 25

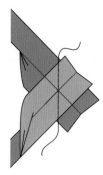

1. Lay binding against quilt to double-check that it is correct length.
2. Trim binding ends, leaving ¹/₄" seam allowance; press seam open. Stitch binding to quilt.
3. Trim backing and batting a scant ¹/₄" larger than quilt top so that batting and backing will fill the binding when it is folded over to quilt backing.
4. On 1 edge of quilt, fold binding over to quilt backing and pin pressed edge in place, covering stitching line (**Fig. 26**). On adjacent side, fold binding over, forming a mitered corner (**Fig. 27**). Repeat to pin remainder of binding in place.

Fig. 26   **Fig. 27**

5. Blindstitch binding to backing, taking care not to stitch through to front of quilt.

HAND STITCHES

BLANKET STITCH
Come up at 1, go down at 2, and come up at 3, keeping thread below point of needle (**Fig. 28**). Continue working as shown in **Fig. 29**.

Fig. 28   **Fig. 29**

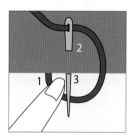   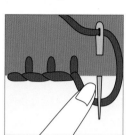

BLIND STITCH
Come up at 1, go down at 2, and come up at 3 (**Fig. 30**). Length of stitches may be varied as desired.

Fig. 30

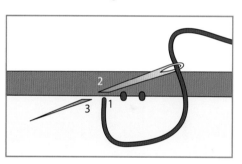

SIGNING AND DATING YOUR QUILT

A completed quilt is a work of art and should be signed and dated. There are many different ways to do this and numerous books on the subject. The label should reflect the style of the quilt, the occasion or person for which it was made, and the quilter's own particular talents. Following are suggestions for recording the history of the quilt or adding a sentiment for future generations.

- Embroider quilter's name, date, and any additional information on quilt top or backing. Matching floss, such as cream floss on white border, will leave a subtle record. Bright or contrasting floss will make the information stand out.

- Make label from muslin and use permanent marker to write information. Use different colored permanent markers to make label more decorative. Stitch label to back of quilt.

- Use photo-transfer paper to add image to white or cream fabric label. Stitch label to back of quilt.

- Piece an extra block from quilt top pattern to use as label. Add information with permanent fabric pen. Appliqué block to back of quilt.

- Write message on appliquéd design from quilt top. Attach appliqué to back of the quilt.

Metric Conversion Chart

Inches x 2.54 = centimeters (cm)	Yards x .9144 = meters (m)
Inches x 25.4 = millimeters (mm)	Yards x 91.44 = centimeters (cm)
Inches x .0254 = meters (m)	Centimeters x .3937 = inches (")
	Meters x 1.0936 = yards (yd)

Standard Equivalents

$1/8$"	3.2 mm	0.32 cm	$1/8$ yard	11.43 cm	0.11 m
$1/4$"	6.35 mm	0.635 cm	$1/4$ yard	22.86 cm	0.23 m
$3/8$"	9.5 mm	0.95 cm	$3/8$ yard	34.29 cm	0.34 m
$1/2$"	12.7 mm	1.27 cm	$1/2$ yard	45.72 cm	0.46 m
$5/8$"	15.9 mm	1.59 cm	$5/8$ yard	57.15 cm	0.57 m
$3/4$"	19.1 mm	1.91 cm	$3/4$ yard	68.58 cm	0.69 m
$7/8$"	22.2 mm	2.22 cm	$7/8$ yard	80 cm	0.8 m
1 "	25.4 mm	2.54 cm	1 yard	91.44 cm	0.91 m

Production Team: Technical Writer - Lisa Lancaster; Technical Associate - Jean Lewis; Editorial Writer - Susan Frantz Wiles ; Senior Graphic Artist - Lora Puls; and Graphic Artist - Victoria Temple.